CHAMORRITA SONG

Volume 99

Sun Tracks

Danielle P. Williams

CHAMORRITA SONG

THE UNIVERSITY OF
ARIZONA PRESS
TUCSON

The University of Arizona Press
www.uapress.arizona.edu

We respectfully acknowledge the University of Arizona is on the land and territories of Indigenous peoples. Today, Arizona is home to twenty-two federally recognized tribes, with Tucson being home to the O'odham and the Yaqui. The University strives to build sustainable relationships with sovereign Native Nations and Indigenous communities through education offerings, partnerships, and community service.

ISBN-13: 978-0-8165-5516-1 (paperback)
ISBN-13: 978-0-8165-5517-8 (ebook)

Cover design by Leigh McDonald
Cover art by Danielle P. Williams
Designed and typeset by Leigh McDonald in Horley Old Style 10.5/14 and Costa (display)

Publication of this book is made possible in part by the proceeds of a permanent endowment created with the assistance of a Challenge Grant from the National Endowment for the Humanities, a federal agency.

Library of Congress Cataloging-in-Publication Data
Names: Williams, Danielle P., author.
Title: Chamorrita song / Danielle P. Williams.
Other titles: Sun tracks ; v. 99.
Description: [Tucson] : University of Arizona Press, 2026. | Series: Sun tracks ; volume 99
Identifiers: LCCN 2025012890 (print) | LCCN 2025012891 (ebook) | ISBN 9780816555161 (paperback) | ISBN 9780816555178 (ebook)
Subjects: LCGFT: Poetry.
Classification: LCC PS3623.I5564934 C47 2026 (print) | LCC PS3623.I5564934 (ebook)
LC record available at https://lccn.loc.gov/2025012890
LC ebook record available at https://lccn.loc.gov/2025012891

Printed in the United States of America
♾ This paper meets the requirements of ANSI/NISO Z39.48-1992 (Permanence of Paper).

"[We know that] to be a brown girl is to call the ocean is to call to the self is to know you have to find a way."

—Barbara Jane Reyes

CONTENTS

CHAMORRITA SONG

WHENEVER I TELL THIS STORY

Whenever I tell this story, I emphasize me, still new in many ways. I emphasize the poems I have written. The ones I have yet to conceive. The ways I use my voice as a guiding point. Home has always been embedded in my bones. It lives freely in the ways I choose to put blood to page. The words that drag out the hurt in me. And these songs echo. Won't someone listen?

THE VALLEY OF THE LATTE

This is the first time I see Guåhan this way.
I feel the heat of August on my skin as our boat

bides along Talofofo and Ugum. Two villages, one river.
The calm middle between jungle and ancestry.

I lie and say that I'm a resident
to get the local entry price.

What I really mean to say is
I am native.

But $45 is better than $90, and I've already
paid my weight in loss.

We glide through the water and throw breadcrumbs
to bait greedy, plump clusters of catfish.

Our guide weaves a tiara of palms
He places it on my head, then weaves a rose,

places it in my left hand. I look up and gush
at the wildlife terrain. Such lush green tropics

swelling into the sky. Weaving past and
present right in front of my eyes.

My cousin tells me that she tries to visit once a year,
that it helps her feel closer to our ancestors.

As we approach the CHamoru village, I am taught
how to ask the taotaomona for permission:

Guella yan guello kao siña hu maloffan gi tano-miyu?
Ancestors, can I pass through your land?

We step off the boat and watch as canoes are hand-
crafted by Ulitao. Men in lavalavas, bare skin to

show us what they're made of. They show us
weaving like I've never seen before:

kottot rice gift baskets, balagbag fanny pack baskets.
Hagug for your voyage off island, the CHamoru

Tupperware of baskets. Baskets like crowns
on the heads of women. We're taught how

to make fire. How it starts from palm and stone.
We see the ancient latte stones lined up and

parallel as if to say *you can thrive here*.
It is in this moment I realize these stones shape people.

Our people.

Our latte stones show us where we began
Passing to the next life within, and around

These stones are shelter, altar, and home.
Cratered limestone clutched in my hand, like

coral, or something that used to be.

KANTAN CHAMORRITA

i.
here are the rules
show up to the center of the village with a sharp tongue
have your friends and family crowd you like graduation day
identify your opponent   be sure   start first
each round compose couplets   yell quatrains
four lines to expel against the forgiving   sea
another opportunity to configure   wit   rhyme   or not
just make sure   it's something   not worth   forgetting
please   don't forget it
your last line can be   anything   but think fast
listen   and   watch as the stories run   straight to you
start your next poem   on your opponent's   last   wish

ii.
once you've got a rhythm about you
and you're crafting songs   pushing fear to the
edge of the village   to the   edge of the
world   don't stop   stop getting in your own way
make sure they remember   our names   show up to the
center   of each room   with a sharp tongue
have your family and friends   hold   your poems like
they should have   held you   your last line   can be
a relief   just make sure there's more
four more poems   means   four more   gone
stories you try   to forget   just four more
be sure to   strike first

iii.
sometimes rhymes are like
uppercuts   *find a life in this chaos*   *make it*
beautiful   start your next poem   with your opponent's last
breath   never forget

iv.

your poems decide what's next

BLACK BODY AS [ ]BIRD

black body as songbird
singing every damn
song but my own
carry me across the sea
make me a seabird
see what they've done to me?
they done made me into somethin' else
now i don't know which sea is home
am i even a bird anymore?
have you seen
what they're doing to me?
black body as bird as
metaphor as song
meant as warning
i'm warning you
let me fly at liberty
let me fly at all
black body said i don't know
which sea is home
songbird can you sing us home?
birds and black bodies born
with wings but don't mean we're
free to go as we please
please, let our bodies be!
they said we're songbirds
got this blues building but can't
nobody hear us speak
black body as songbird
as seabird
is it a song?
is it a body at all?
is there a home we can call our own?
more like those cursed blackbirds

more like death to black bodies
and their dreams
can't none of us really leave
black bodies with this
colonized disease ain't no-
body 'bout ain't to hear our songs
noways

THE FA'ÑAGUE IN AMERICA

i.
in america
hardly anyone knows
i'm a *chamorrita*
they know little of
guam or saipan
know nothing of how the
hell we're supposed to dance
around america's world
to imagine life with littered roots
there's *taotaomona* in the bodies of
black girls but they don't know
how to be in two places at once
they don't know how to be
american and remain calmly
in their own skin
in a land they do not own

ii.
america
knowing little
of the feeling
of gender let alone
a way to describe it
casting labels but
lacking detail
colonizing everything yet
misunderstanding simple concepts
queerness was never meant to stay quiet
history can't be repeated without inspiration
we were matriarchs in our marianas
we were naked and free
and without shame

sacred vessels
stories passed down
instinctual
everything that was
everything that is

iii.
in america
the natives of our
oceans get reduced to
backslash
categories not big enough
to hold our seas
shining in the ambers
of our ancestors
we will rise with the tide
dream and gleam and
reap our majesties

iv.
at my auntie's home
in hawai'i where our bloodline
also lives the wind
welcomes her wise words
she says it so simply
never turn your back to the ocean
oh the sea and its unpredictability
oh the shining nature of forcing a way
and claiming what you feel is owed

CHAMORRITA SONG

every now and then
i try to write a poem like
my ancestors would have
i recite my words feel the

gravity of my grief
i feel theirs too
i am only a quatrain away
from something that understands

me better than me
my poem standing tall
a shield to cover my bare bones
a poem can be home

it protects me
and every now and then
i imagine faces like mine
the kinds of poems i'd find

GOSPEL

the first
gospel song

was a slave song

knees hinged
in cotton

fields

palms propped
pricked & calloused

begging for
mercy

mercy

meant
something

different

our god
took life

and death
too

literally
lacked miracle
miracle

meant
something

different

our songs
saved us

they never stopped
pouring

out of our
dry mouths

sun anointing

our backs
as we labored

our chorus
an echo

of us big
bellows of

brown tremor

trauma echoed
and called back

prayers

to our god
with skin like soil

we're still
searching

searching

for answers
in gospels

we soon realize

miracles
life itself

started in our own bones

our songs
god's gospel

humming heavy
in our veins

hear us everywhere

COMPETING WITH MYSELF

our villages gather at noon
wait for competing wit

people with burdens to lay
down and anger to spit:

I am the competitor
the poet

the teller of this story
I write about how waves carry my worry

it's in my own hands now
and don't we all have our own

kitchens to sweep free of sand and salt
aren't we all begging for freedom

I stare at my opponent
examine their pride sitting like a belt

hanging on a hinged hip like a heavy legacy
we know that this battle is one version of a destiny

the wind blows and these songs go
kantan i lina'la i taotao-tano

these are the songs of the people
wailing away at the sea

FOR HIDING LOVE FROM OTHERS

Ya malago' yu na hu tungo'
Manu nai gaige piniti-mu;
Kao i trongkon korason-mu,
Pat i pintan babli-mu.

//

i would like to know where
you store your love pains
at the pit of your heart?
at the ends of your lashes?

    i'm cratered wall
    all limestone and stubbornness
    this love is big and hurts
    but it is my burden alone

and I'm still
falling
fading into
waves' foam

and nobody told
me how to love
only how not
to die

in my pit
in my rigid
core I'm still
waiting for you

but I can't
love you
i can't even
love myself

//

FA'ÑAGUE /FUH-NYAH-GWEE/

1. a person or
   place habitually frequented;

   // a presence entering the
   questioning of your dreams

   // the way the breeze whispers
   through the coconut trees
   in your aunt's backyard

   // the shrieking panic coming from the
   chickens that wakes you up at 4 a.m.

   // the danger in turning your back to the sea

2. the action or power of being
   haunted;

   // a shadow along the
   lining of my skin

   // where your past and
   present selves begin

   // an attachment; a belonging; a becoming

3. the haunting;

   // the taotaomona, aniti; the people before time, the
   spirits of our same name

   // the strength in realizing superstition lives
   the life you're afraid to

4. an awakening;

// when a person returns home to Guåhan; to
Saipan; to whatever islands are
embedded in their dna they begin
to feel whole again

I couldn't feel you before this—where have you been?

WHEN PEOPLE TELL ME THAT DANCING HULA MAKES YOU EXOTIC

people tell

me
          dancing hula

makes   you   *exotic*

they don't know   what   it means

when my nana   points her palms

                    purposefully and

                                        sharp

they've never felt

          felt

          felt

real blades   seen   seen   seen

a father   his body

          collapsed   hips

hidden   hidden   machete

          machete   machete on the

slant

of his crinkled-over neck

when my nana dances   she's praying

she's dancing the story of her father

her father

her father   not yet beheaded   amen

thank you god   ai adai!   ai adai!   ai adai!

as her hands guide   her eyes   to the sky

the sky

the sky

the sky   is all he saw before his forehead hit the

cold wet dirt

then those boots   the japanese   soldiers   the sky

of Guåhan   native land   her feet moving

ever so slightly

· her chin down

staring at the

ground

instead of cutting my great   tata's head off   the soldiers pulled

out their   dicks

and pissed

on his weeping face
mace

mace

mace

that's the word   in english   my nana never

learned

though

she translated it   her sad sad hula   the image of her

father dead

dead   in more ways than one

her mother and brothers and sisters

kneeling down behind him

praying to god   waiting

for his   execution

ai adai   ai adai   god

ai adai   my god!

what you don't know

is that hula   is trauma   expressed through the body

a dance   to relive   to outlive   to set free   to cry

cry

cry

and live many lives   not your own
and you can't

not dance

and you can't not

remember what haunts you

CHAMORRITA SONG

fighting rage   and winning   trying to find the best way
to categorize your pain   to know when it's time to
cry yourself a new poem   tell the world about yourself
again   break down   on your knees   begging in Garamond
twelve-point font   pounding   your fingers to the pavement
of your rose-gold MacBook Air   remember all the ways
your mother-father-brother   family in everything but the
sense of this curious word   cut into your skin   you question
where your life begins   & a new poem   is like a new
friend just getting to know you   just waiting for the line
or stanza that practically breaks you   just waiting to meet you at the
end   and hold what hurts

STEAL AWAY

If you want to find Jesus, go in the wilderness,
[You want to find Jesus,] Go in the wilderness,

//

if you want to find Jesus
be wilderness be wild
[you want to find religion,]
get out of your body and into the whipping breeze
backslide into the parts of you
not bound be free like
days without chains or ticking seconds
so you want to know God?
[*'flicted sister,* have you no shame?]
half-done Christian God ain't no name
Jesus a waitin' to meet you in de wilderness
ancestors a waitin' to meet you in the flesh
who will you choose?

//

CREATION MYTH

i. Puntan
come
sister pluck
out my
eyes queue
sun and
moon draw
blueprints from
my breast break
ground from
my back
lend the
arch of my
brow to
rainbows
give the
clouds their
thickness
just think
what artistry

o sister
my Fu'uña
listen
to my dreams
help me
greet death
make new
breath of
my last
let me feel
what it is
to become

ii. Fu'uña
my Puntan
my world
i will make
your death
beautiful
o brother
what sadness
what wishes
what is my life
without you?

just as you
have proclaimed
i promise
to create
many pairs
in your honor
brothers and
sisters alike
what love

i will lay
my body down
turn to
stone
spread
my life on
uninhabited
terrain
join
the sky
let our
people
feel us
as the breeze
through
love

our weeping
hearts
a lifeline
legacies of
your skin
in death
is where we exist

FOR FISHING

Ti gumadi yu' put ti'ao
Na gumadi yu' put hagu
An' chumefla yu' tres biahi
Yute' gadi ya'un falagu.

//

i'm not fishing for small fish
net cast wide as the sea
count to three wade whistle wait
someone will come for me

who's to say you'll be found
who's to say anything is out there
come to terms, come to your senses
come feel the island air on you

oh to
feel
the tide
against
my toes

to know
in my
heart
there is
someone
there's beauty in thought
you think over
and over to yourself:
here

is where love

can live
withstand the waves   restore the sea
sometimes   you forget   the tide takes
more
than it gives

//

CRYSTAL STAIR

after Langston Hughes

i.
Well   Daughter
I'll tell you life for me ain't been a life at all
                    It's had bullets in it, and bullies, and
                        Haters and places with no carpet
Bare
And all the time   I'm breathing   And cursing the sky
    And wondering why women like us   Don't get saved
                    There ain't no light

Just Black girls gettin' snatched in the dark
                Ain't nobody savin' us

    Daughter   Save yourself first   Don't you turn back

I'm telling you life for me ain't been no crystal stair
                Life for me ain't been a life at all
                                But I'm still goin'
                        Honey

ii.
Well   Mother
I don't know where to exist in this life
    I've learned
Life is what we make it   Plus Black skin
It's had its tacks in it   And splinters   And boards torn up
    And I don't think I've ever actually seen   A finished home

    Or floors with carpet
You taught me to always keep going
    My mother   Honey   and hue
Magic that men   Don't understand
Life for us   Will never be   A crystal stair
But we build our own   damn houses

WHEN PEOPLE ASK ME WHAT I AM INSTEAD OF WHO

I'm a Black girl
    a Chamorrita
Flesh and bone
    curl and coconut oil

Brutal and honest but silent as
    dust settling on ceiling fans
A thing of decoration
    a way of completing a room

A mother's daughter
    Matanane and Brown
        Manglona and Williams
Something my ancestors dreamed

I think
    I'm a dream too
Someone's last wish
    a history of sorts

Some call me modern-day storyteller
    a villager reciting my angst
Against the sea   ripping apart and
    coming together again with my unsung words

I am many half-written poems in
    bodies of water my body cannot store properly
Poems and songs and psalms all of which
    make my hips shake and ache

Catch me wandering to the altar
after the call
A new believer
hymnal turned remix and lives made whole

With ears ready to listen to church break-
downs lasting twenty whole minutes if you act right
A moment of joy hinged on my
knees and prayer hands

Reprise in the form of flesh

FOR DAUGHTERS

I recall the gold
expandable bracelet that

once rested between the
rolls on my fat baby wrist.

Gold flowers and vine adorning
the curve. As I grew, it opened

to welcome the years, an expanding
clasp, another version awaiting the

woman in me. And when my bones
were finally too big for baby trinkets,

my nana and mom handed me a
new bracelet in a pink drawstring pouch

with pink flowers and vines adorning
the lining. Another bracelet lost with

Engravings I can't remember. Gifts
that we somehow always knew

came from home. I left
the island just as I was old

enough to speak back with
Chamorro on my tongue.

There are only so many things
that can be translated.

Only so many ways to sit and toil
and think about a home you've had

so little time to grow into.

FOR PLACES WE'VE NEVER BEEN BUT DREAM OF GOING TO ONCE WE DIE

Ma susede un desgråsia
as Malilok na lugåt.
Ya ti ilek-ho na ti un måtai,
na un måtai naturåt.

//

have you heard of the misfortune
at a place called Malilok?
i never said you would never die
only that death would come naturally

    a soul transformed
    a life of storms
    you should know by now
    everything dies

like the new tide
        there then gone
and Malilok
        was my last sight

    a beauty to behold
                for the last time
            i let the water carry   me softly
                        deliver me
                                        to the
                        light

there's always
something

grinding its way
to death

//

\\ RETURNING \\

back to myself

returning home
it's been a long
time gone

it's been many lives

clawing flesh
breaking skin
raging to be

more than memory

and i am many lives

and each day
i write a new poem
study a new ache

my body
a graveyard
a familial obligation
a way of translating

what it means
when they say

it's not over until it's over

CREATION MYTH

after Langston Hughes

i've known the sea
i've known seas as old as
        the sky and its freckled stars

my soul has grown deep like the sea

and us two   we bathed in the glory of great power   we were

young before we were   artifact   my dear brother

you made me   promise to use you:

make our people from me   build seas from my   beating heart   still

i heard this   singing in your dying   breath   then raised
        the world   is you   at sunset
        i'm waves   against the   horizon

i've known the sea:
my brother   and me

my soul has grown deep like the sea

FOR MOTHERS

any foreign mother knows america
has its own fees / so do we / the children
the slow erasure / the vessels crossing many
seas / these high tides strong like rush hour high-
ways to nowhere / which way is america? / how long
'til water becomes dirt? / 'til the journey brings us
to safety? / safely? / we've been promised / lives / land
there is a trigger- / fish stretched over saipan
trace the points along its body / let the rising and
setting stars become a guide / find whatever it is that
serves you / in america / being a color / not white / is like
serving time / chain bolted to feet bolted to ground
the ash of dust / collecting at your ankles / the sound
of the waves / so close / so close / how long 'til dirt becomes grave?

any foreign mother will point / you / to the wall
closest to the door / motion for you to take off your shoes
in her home / my own / mother / is a complicated woman
for most of our lives / we have been foreign / to one another
watching from afar / biding / waiting for a place to call
our own / we live on the surface / drown with our
backs turned / who knows what we yearn / I don't
know her well / she doesn't know / me / I am a rogue
wave / my own way / I am destruction / sometimes
I am / saving lives / my own way / writing away
from the chaos / from the blood / that bonds us
sometimes / I am afraid / to ask / what haunts you?
sometimes / I am afraid / that / you / won't / bring yourself
to show me / you / at my home / there is a mat at the door / for shoes

FOR MOTHERS PT. 2

Basta nana de tumanges
Saosao todu i lago'-mu
Sa' ti u apmam na tiempo
Siempre u fatto i lahi-mu

//

mothers stop your crying
wipe worry clean from your eyes
it won't be long now
your sons are near

        war means months since i've seen his face
        prayers are the only thing that soothe me
        i send them up and out and hope
        he returns with the sea

villages   of sons
             sent to fight for land   they'll never see

        villages   of mothers
                     without sons
                                 weathered cemeteries
                                              to weep in

//

STEAL AWAY

Steal away to Jesus,
Steal away home,
I hain't got long to stay here.

//

Meet me at our secret place
I ain't got long so steal away

Time ain't on our side so steal
away before we get stole

Sing our song sweetly
A-tremblin' in our black bones

We poor sinners singing so
Maybe one day we can go home

I wait upon de Lord, my God,
Who take away de sin of the world.

Tell me is God on his way?

//

ANYONE WHO DOES NOT KNOW LOVE IS STILL IN DEATH

after bell hooks

when i think about love
i imagine bells, sonic hooks

sounds used to catch things

i imagine sirens
swimming the sea

waiting for someone
to get close enough to love

imagine living with the intent
to love a love

imagine being so far
then so close then nothing

still dancing and swimming
with hope on your back

then nothing

when i think about love
i think about what it is not

how all my life
people have tried and failed

how words like
nice and *sweet* and *love* are nothing

without action

my own mother couldn't
love me the way i needed
and sometimes i imagine
it having nothing to do with me

that maybe this whole time
she's just been living and bleeding

living with the intent
to love a love

being so far then so close
then nothing

still dancing and swimming
with hope on her back

then nothing

i sometimes think
maybe she's never
really lived

wonder without a living life
how one loves anything?

wonder how a mother can love
a daughter in death?

WHEN PEOPLE DON'T CARE TO LEARN THE DIFFERENCE BETWEEN US

has your skin not
turned to ash

are you not
gripping the sand

sinking dead by
your own damn land

can you blink
away this pain

is there a box in you
that locks away the

things you once loved

I once loved a man who
would joke about my mom:

she's Asian it's all the same
I'm so goddamn tired of being erased

I once loved a woman who
took everything too seriously

even my laughter wasn't safe
my softness

the way i clung to memory
called it a kind of gospel
the pain inside me
impossible

my life reiterates
in my tiny five-two frame

my ancestors swell in my blood
how could others ever truly understand

how to exude a name
how to surpass a world of words

that claim your soul
I wonder

can these waves carry me away
can they find me refuge

can these songs
the hum of the wind

slapping dead at the sea
what rage and

ignorance and
are you not

overwhelmed by it
do you not beg for

release

TANO I' MAN CHAMORRO

Tano I' Man Chamorro   *but who am I really?*
I was once described as   a half breed   I was once described as
    royalty
my nana used to tell me   I was the sea   free to be anything   or
    anywhere
that I was the allowance   of   new people to   new places
                                        the ebb
                                        and flow
                                        of cultures
                                    unknown
the last time I visited Saipan   my elders told me I looked like them
they described many taotaomona bearing our name
                                    traced their fingers
                                to my features   and
                                applauded the continuance
                                of a culture that was told to
                                be dying
I remember   smiling   at the few words I could make out
    I remember   wondering   what life would be like if my
grandparents had   passed on the language   instead
    of leaving us to feel   like strangers in the midst of   family
I was once described as   poison
I was once described as   anointed
my poison comes from my *tainted* blood   with a name not given by
this land
    I take to my feet   to the sand   my hands   crescents
        curved to the sky   tell my story through palms and
    weary hips   I sometimes feel the aniti on me   they tell their
        stories through my poems   I'm told that means I
    am chosen
they come to me in dreams   in waves   of emotion
    with my eyes wide open   and curious and   they tell me
prophecies   issue warnings   wish me

well   whisper things in the night   I must   decipher   I'm
an oracle   a last resort
and my ancestors   are long buried but   still visit   like
the tide
        Tano' I Man Chamorro   *but who am I really?*
my nana used to tell me   I was the
                                        sea

FOR THE CHAINS I BREAK FREE FROM

Yanggen lulok bai hu hulok,
an kadena bai desåse.
Bai atotga bumusero
yanggen gaige hao fondon tåse.

//

give me iron and watch me break it
chain me and watch it come undone
i'm a dared diver roaming
find me free at the bottom

        i will master your trials
        move heaven and earth to make way
        i will find what you've hidden
        search each end of the world

you better have

                better weapons than iron

for i am fire
                and you

                        have kept me long enough

//

BEAR IN MIND THAT DEATH IS A DRUM

after Langston Hughes

Do you feel that violent
bumping in your body?

The rhythm of your
Life bolting from itself

The syncopation of your heartbeat
Drumming up death

And how are you not
Jumping out of your bones?

Stomping for God or
Second chances

When it comes for me
I'll be damned if i'm not dancing

They say if you dance good enough
The holy ghost can catch you

Carry you to a new home
Worth living for

Meantime we're still here
Still dancing

Awaiting death like altar call

Listening to life like a
Signal to start the song

And when the drums roll for me
And boom cats a groove worth dancing for
Worth dying for

I'll be here
Waiting at God's door

FOR THE CHILDREN TALKING TO US IN HEAVEN

Båsta nåna de tumånges
sa' un na' lache karerå-ho;
yan maolek-ña yo' gi langet
ke i tano' na sagå-ho.

//

mother   stop your crying
your prayers are loud
but i am on god's path
in heaven where love forever lasts

    daughter calm these swells
    my eyes red with high tide
    redirect my pain
    take away the rain

    //

DEVOTIONAL

my mom
hardly cries
though she
prays
beads falling
like tears
delivered
straight to god
we cannot stray
our path is
low tide
footprints cement
like ocean brick
sometimes
it seems like
her prayers
could reach out and
slap me

DEEP RIVER

Deep River, my house is over Jordan, Deep River,
Lord, I want to cross over into campground;

//

Deep River, unbound Sea, Deep River
Lord, I want to cross over into thee;

deep river
my house
is over
Jordan
deep river
this is
not where
i'm meant
to be
my home
is an ocean
away
deep
rivers my
body
is a boat
my soul
floats on
camp's edge
i'm first to
fledge
first to free
myself
unbound
like the

deep river
deep sea
cross over
and believe

//

GOD / GÄD /

1. / when imposed / the creator and ruler,
the source of all m/oral/ authority;
the supreme being
/ anyone but us /

// a person, or thing of supreme value
what does value mean in
damned prayers?

// take it or leave it. leave
and be lost

are you a demon or a god?

2. in certain other religions / like the ones they've long buried /
a superhuman
a powerful spirit willing the worlds.

// how do i know if you're safe to
follow what follows
am i still my own version of me
will you change me for the better or
am i better off alone

// when i think about "god" i imagine
women dancing naked in the sun.
god, what did i do to deserve this?

exclamation

1. used for emphasis or to express emotions such as surprise, anger, or distress

SUGAR KING PARK, SAIPAN

there seems to be   a trend   in thievery
a reaping   of sacred lands   hands in the
dirt   harvesting   crops   and hearts   and   other things

we lost   so many lives   to outsiders   thinking
they know better   and now   our children have   cavities and
we spent   too many years   numbing   their pain
goddamn   sugar cane   goddamn   sugar cane
come cry in nana's bosom   child   come   listen   to the waves

fall asleep   and i'll rage   i'll question   the moon
when i give   my child   to the sea   what   will come of them?

CHAMORRITA SONG

sometimes
i hate myself
for forgetting
what Chamorro

sounds like on
the tongue
and i try
to think real hard

imagine my aunties
laughing about their lives
yelling to their kids
grandkids *neni girl*

and i need to hear
what comes
next but
can't

i want to be
in two languages
at once
but can't

sometimes
i hate
my mom
and her parents too

just for a second
when i'm grasping
at straws

searching my memory

i hate
that nobody
thinks
about me

that nobody
figured i'd want
to know them
in this way too

FOR THE CHILDREN WHO ROT AWAY, SLOWLY

An tumåtånges i patgon
nå'e na'-ña entot tupu.
Yanggen sige ha' de tumånges,
håtsa hulo' ya un na' susu.

//

when tears fall from your children
plump their gums with sugar cane
cushion their fears / make them feel love again
offer them everything   / your bosom as comfort

when the waves rage   we cry
tears soften into your ocean of arms
will morning follow night?
does a mother rage when provoked?

//

YUTU 2018

I
think
often

about
bodies
that

aren't
mine

swells
of blue bullies

crashing into
one another

shadows
over

neighbors
homes like

an anxious
reaper

my
nana is

a perfect
example

of how
us

Chamorro are
not easily

broken
the waves

come
and go

and we are
always thankful

for what reminds
us of

lands our
ancestors

willed

this summer I
finally learned

what it feels
like to

know
you
can't
get lost

somewhere
with only

three roads
I wonder

if anyone
else in the

world knows
after Yutu hit

my family went
three months

without
power

the ocean
is a mighty

mighty body
pulsing

in the pit of
our design

reef and
rubble in our

lungs

why is it
we love

the things
that hurt us

I wonder
if anyone else

on this earth
knows

we were born
from water

they
can never

truly
erase us

FOR ALL THE TIME THAT HAS GONE BY

Antes gi annai tiempo-mu
Kalan makina hao ni' bibu
Annai esta ti tiempo-mu
Kalan puyitos manok hao ni' figo.

//

time was once yours

fast and always moving forward

now gone

you're the shivering chick watching in horror

  i held time in my hands

    i felt too much too fast

  i hoped maybe someone somewhere

    could bring to time what i lacked

we are not given
time for second
chances

we are not given
the lives we're
meant to live

we watch time
moving away
from us

we are lost
in the world
that remade us

what in the world
do i do
with wiped palms

a gentle touch
to always miss
we should be remiss

there will always
be people racing
to see who can
destroy you first

and no matter how
far back or how far
into forward you
venture there are

always gatekeepers
racing to kill you
first don't you see
your worth

you're less alive
to some people
if you're not white
you're a delusion

a mirage
of miracles
not meant for them
to fathom

//

DEEP RIVER

I am huntin' [see] for a city, [home] so stay awhile,
O Believer [Po'sinner] got a home at las['.]

//

I am dreamin' [home] in this city, [can] I stay awhile,
I am hunted [see] for a city, [can] I stay awhile,

O Redeamer [Po'sinner] she ain't never goin' back[!]
[Po'sinner] dreamin' [home] she ain't never goin' back[!]

> *O brothers, don't get weary,*
> *[Us] We're waiting for the Lord.*
>
> *When we [us] land on Canaan's shore,*
> *[Us] We'll meet forever more.*
>
> > O sisters, free your worry,
> > [Us] We're waiting for the Lord,
> >
> > [Us] We've never been more sure,
> > When we [us] land on Canaan's shore,
> >
> > [Us] We'll be free forever more.
> > O Redeamer I am dreaming of [forever].
>
> //

BLACK MUSIC

I feel music all over my body.
Like hives, or hiccups.
Like Jesus. Two parted
hands waitin' to be met
by the downbeat.

I'm all double claps &
church stomp. Holy
ghosts & hallelujah.
I feel it & off my feet go
& the church aunties in
the back they shoutin':

Let the spirit take you chile!

& I'm took. My body is the
good book. It's hymnal.
It's sacrifice.

Let the spirit take you chile!

& I remember readin'
somethin' about a
resurrection &

Ain't God good!

I've gotten good at going
to church now
& I feel it when I'm
singing & dancin' in them
pews, but someone
tell me, what becomes

of my body when
the music stops?

Let the spirit take you chile!

And this ain't the first time
I've been taken without
being ready to go
as if God doesn't know
!

CHAMORRITA SONG

Sometimes I imagine I am a competitor
That I have a say in what happens to my body

That I'm not just anybody
That I'm a poet

All rhyme and song and beating heart
A body like water ripping life apart

Each word a gospel
Each return another chance to fight for my life

I think I deserve that right

And there's nothing new about these songs

Just like my hands still bleed

I've learned we're not who people believe
But I still yell my poems like last words

I still hope for relief

ALL THE OCEAN

I tasi lumalalai minagof guatu gi as Yu'os
I tasi bumabaila minagof guatu gi as Yu'os
                                        The ocean sings for the joy of the Lord
                                        The ocean dances for the joy of the Lord
I tasi lumalalai   and so I sing
I tasi bumabaila   and so I dance
I tano I man Chamorro   and so I am   the land   too
I am native   to these waves
The joy in the heart of low tide
               a strong body
               a heavy retreat
I bring as much of me back   as the Lord allows me   as
Yu'os   as Yu'os
I tasi bumabaila   I dance and I feel like home   I tasi   I tasi
I tasi   the ocean   the ocean it may drown me   but   but   but

I never die   I tasi
I tasi   the ocean   the ocean   all the ocean   it could claim me
and   I would not care
I tasi   lumalalai   bumabaila   sing   dance   lumalalai
bumabaila   sing   dance
live   live   in water where my sins   could never be
minagof guatu gi as Yu'os
baptize me   taotao   I tasi   I am from the ocean   all the
ocean   Yu'os   wash me   of my pain
make me   new again

FOR WHAT'S FELT IN THE BODY

there's this
almost / unspeakable
low / whisper / a throb / buzzing
in your back

a return / to moments
you'd / never / wish / on anyone
this silent / choke / grabbing
hold / quietly / taking everything

and there's just / enough / life
left in / you / to scream / but you don't
you just / feel / the cage of your body
wish it gone

wish / it didn't look / so much like you
wish / it tried harder / for an ounce of familiarity

//

sometimes with death
ash / pummels / into grave / like
life's blunt / ashing / on the lands
of you/r/ ancestors

you have to / save yourself / first
worry the soul- / talk / for the days
you're / no longer / here to keep
explaining your pain / away

this / is what's / felt / in the body
to / cradle yourself / anew

CHAMORRITA SONG

for me, my sister, my mother, and my mother's mother

it has taken time to cry
to live outside of yourself
to know how to belong to what was
once ripped from your own body

your baby is a poet now
she is telling you it is okay
she is reading you her life's work
showing you how life has worked her

it has taken time to cry
but here you are
two bodies
two daughters

only ever wishing
to know their mothers

it is hard to admit
what distance does

it is easier
to cry in the arms

of what confuses you most
of who loves you most

WHEN WE TALK ABOUT DREAMING

i can feel hundreds of
hands laid on the blades

of my shoulders like
latte stones weighing into

sand / sanctuary / burden
never forget where you come from

weight so heavy my knees creak
a deep-breezed hum / go this way /

and without question
i listen / ékungok /

and though there are
no sounds

/ in a way that can only be described as /
magic / or / birthright /

fa'ñague / filter centuries-old stories
through my consciousness

and my eyes stare blankly
every / which / way

and i hear all of them
one / after / another

in turn / in time
it's almost as if they had been waiting
lifetimes for me to meet them / here

and i want to ask / why me?

but in dreams like this
i am not given a voice / ékungok /

i listen / save the rest for the outside
the questioning

and their words / move me / to feeling
and i feel it all

and i write it all

A NOTE FROM THE AUTHOR

This collection, *Chamorrita Song*, operates as translation and adaptation. Designed to stray from the original *Chamorrita* song and to evolve in parallel with my own understanding of self and my surroundings, it draws directly from ancient Chamorro folk songs. *Chamorrita* song, or *Kantan Chamorrita*, was an impromptu style of verse making that operated as a call-and-response, during which villagers would "throw" verses back and forth like a poetic debate playing out between clans. A competition in the form of quatrains arranged in two couplets was performed until one participant failed to create a new verse. This practice of improvisation and performance, which originated in Black and Indigenous communities struggling under the weight of colonization, is the foundation of this collection. These poems engage with my culture and identity, grasping at and diverging from traditions and demonstrating how people have chosen to turn to music, song, poetry, and dance—as well as other methods of art making—to express their feelings.

My hope is that these poems provide readers with an understanding of how I am grounding myself as the poet, and in a way, as the competitor. I situate readers in a familiar reality, then lead them toward its faceted nuances.

In terms of my identity, some people choose to see only one side of me. This was especially true as I grew up in the South. There is little nuance in defining who you are when the world looks at you and decides for themselves. These poems speak to my distinctions as a queer, Black, and Indigenous woman. My poems are the lens through which I have come to understand my identity within my culture—through the struggles and atrocities that other communities have endured—and these poems have helped me discover what it means to align myself with others in our intricate human existence.

Much of what I've reflected on in these poems comes from conversations with native Chamorro speakers and advocates, family members, and community members, as well as online resources, books, and other texts I consulted while researching at the Micronesian Area Research Center at the University of Guam. When cultures are colonized, there is a wave of erasure resulting in changes to the native tongue, including naming and renaming things to the point where languages can be lost entirely. This speaks to the intentionality of the Chamorro misspellings in my poems. These misspellings represent changes to the Chamorro language that occurred when the Mariana Islands changed colonial hands, as seen in words like *CHamoru*, *Chamorro*, and *Chamoru*, and the lasting impact of colonization. Changes in these Chamorro words mirror changes in terms like *African American*, *colored*, *Negro*, *Black*, and *Black American* in the United States. Both are systems of labeling that exist to limit, rather than extend.

Other traditions of storytelling, like hula, were instrumental to my awareness of culture and community and how that knowledge is brought to life through dance. When my mother's family traveled with the military, she was intentional about finding a hālau hula that included a range of people from across the Pacific islands and helped to foster an understanding of communal similarities and beliefs. My family has carried forward this tradition both recreationally and competitively, passing on an art form that continues to be translated from island to island, adapting it to fit the needs of the community, and grounding lineages living so far away from their original islands.

Instead of demonstrating a single mode of storytelling, the poems in this collection are meant to reflect the adaptability of Chamorro cultural practices. Similarly, the songs of enslaved people have been adapted into modern-day gospel, blues, rock, and R & B—each a different mode of storytelling. It is Chamorro culture's similar ability to adapt its modes of storytelling that brought to life the artful homages (i.e., poems) in this collection. These poems are not about claiming a single cultural practice as my own but rather about illustrating how Black and Indigenous people have used art to express generational trauma from our imposed colonizers for centuries. To this day, we continue to adapt our modes of storytelling and to revel in the beauty of our collective pain—and our triumph—through storytelling.

ACKNOWLEDGMENTS

The author's poems have previously appeared in the following publications:

Indigenous Pacific Islander Eco-Literatures, "fa'ñague /fuh-nyah-gwee/"
Gulf Coast, "Kantan Chamorrita 1–5"
Indiana Review, "When people tell me that dancing hula makes you exotic"
The Pinch, "Black Body as [ ]Bird"
Sinking City, "The Valley of the Latte"
Ninth Letter 2020 Literary Award Winner, "fa'ñague /fuh-nyah-gwee/"
Ninth Letter 2020 Literary Award Winner, "Gospel"
Flypaper Lit, "Yutu 2018"
Kissing Dynamite Poetry, "Bear in mind that death is a drum"
IceFloe Press, "two sonnets / for mothers"
IceFloe Press, "When people ask me what I am instead of who"
IceFloe Press, "All the Ocean"
Cobra Milk, "Black Music"
Third Point Press, "Tano I' Man Chamorro"

ABOUT THE AUTHOR

Danielle P. Williams is a Black and Chamorro poet, translator, essayist, and spoken-word artist from Columbia, South Carolina. She received her BA in arts administration from Elon University in 2016 and her MFA in creative writing from George Mason University in 2021.

She has received nominations for the Pushcart Prize, Best New Poets, Best of the Net, and Best Microfiction. She was the winner of the 2020 *Ninth Letter* Literary Award in Poetry and a finalist for the *Arts & Letters* Rumi Prize for Poetry in 2021. She has attended the Open Mouth Poetry Retreat and holds fellowships from Palm Beach Poetry Festival, The Watering Hole, and The Alan Cheuse International Writers Center, where she was the 2019 MFA travel fellow and traveled to Hawai'i, Guam, and Saipan to help write this collection.

Her chapbook *Who All Gon' Be There?* was a finalist for the Button Poetry Chapbook Contest and was selected as runner-up for the Backbone Press third Annual Chapbook Competition. It was published by Backbone Press in November 2021.

Williams is also the author of a self-published collection of poetry, *The Art in Knowing Me*; two spoken-word EPs, *At My Own Risk* and *We Fall Down*; and one album, *Danielle Paige*, available on all streaming platforms.

She currently lives in Los Angeles, where she works as a copywriter and creative strategist and performs her poetry to anyone who will listen.